Dustbin

Michaela Morgan

Illustrated by Dee Shulman

OXFORD
UNIVERSITY PRESS

1

Hello, Dustbin!

Dylan loved to play in the park with Dustbin, the family dog.

The game they both liked to play was 'Fetch that stick!'

It was Dustbin's favourite game.

The rules of this game are quite simple:

1 The human throws a stick.

2 The dog chases the stick.

3 The dog brings the stick back and chews it. It's an easy game but many dogs get it wrong.

Dustbin is BRILLIANT at this game. He's the star. He loves chewing sticks.

One sunny Saturday, Dylan and Dustbin went to the park. Dustbin liked to meet all the other dogs.

There was Bully and his owner …

… Spotty and her owner …

… Fifi and her owner …

and there was Dustbin and his family.

Some of the other dogs were not very kind to Dustbin. This made Dustbin sad.

Dylan was *always* kind to Dustbin. He had loved Dustbin from the first time they had met.

Both Dylan and Dustbin had been adopted into the family some time ago.

DAD

MUM

SHELLEY
(my sister)

DYLAN
(me)

Dylan was adopted when he was three years old. He was eight now.

Dustbin had been found in a dustbin when he was a little fat puppy. He was a little fat dog now.

Everyone said the same thing about Dustbin:

That dog will chew anything!

chew! chew! chew! chew!

2

Sticky times

One week, Dylan did a project at school.
It was all about healthy eating.

As he learned more and more, Dylan
became more and more worried. He was
worried about Dustbin.

Dustbin did not do healthy eating.
He ate junk food. In fact he ate junk.

If Dustbin saw a bin of rubbish, he ate it. Sometimes he ate the bin too.

As the days passed and the weeks passed and the months passed, Dustbin grew fatter and fatter.

Dylan became more and more worried.

'I think we should take Dustbin to the vet,' said Dylan.

Look at him!

In the end, Mum agreed. So off they went to the vet.

'Hmm ...' said the vet. 'I want you to keep a diary of *everything* Dustbin eats for five days. Then come back and show it to me.'

Dylan kept the diary very carefully.

He took it back to the vet.

She had a long look at it and sighed.

This is the diary:

Monday

2 dishes of dog food and 1 bowl of water
6 biscuits (chocolate)
1 chocolate fudge cake (and its box)
1 shoe (black)

Tuesday

2 dishes of dog food and 1 bowl of water
8 biscuits (jammy)
1 birthday cake (and its candles)
1 chair (small)

Wednesday

2 dishes of dog food and 1 bowl of water
10 biscuits (custard)
1 shopping bag (and shopping)
1 table leg (wooden)

Thursday

2 dishes of dog food and
1 bowl of water
11 biscuits (with pink icing)
1 pizza (and box)
1 straw hat (crunchy)

Friday

2 dishes of dog food and
1 bowl of water
22 biscuits (mixed)
1 pillow
1 pair of underpants
1 wellington boot (chewy)
3 socks (smelly)

13

The vet read all this out. Then she sighed again. 'This is not healthy food,' she said.

Dylan had to agree.

Even Dustbin looked a bit ashamed of himself.

Burp!
Oops!
Pardon!

FOR CATS ONLY

'From now on,' the vet said, 'this dog is only allowed to have ONE dish of *healthy* dog food every day. He can have as much water as he wants. But he can have NOTHING else.

If he likes chewing, let him chew sticks. They will keep his teeth healthy and sharp.'

Dylan nodded. 'And,' the vet added, 'you must give him lots of exercise!'

'I will,' Dylan promised.

3

Exercise!

All the family tried to keep Dustbin away from unhealthy food.

Dylan took Dustbin for walks and for runs ... and swimming.

It wasn't easy, but, bit by bit, Dustbin became healthier and healthier.

His fur started to shine. His eyes started to glow. His teeth started to gleam.

gleam

On Sunday, all the family went out to the woods with Dustbin. First they played 'Fetch that stick'. Then they played 'Race the stick' in the stream. Dustbin loved that.

Then they decided to play 'Hide and Seek'.

Dustbin wasn't keen on this game, so he lay down and chewed his sticks happily.

Mum counted up to a hundred.

Dad and Dylan and Shelley ran off to hide.

4

Dustbin gets chewing

Dylan wanted to find a
really good hiding place.
Then he remembered
that when he was little,
he had played in an old
hollow tree.

'*That's* a good hiding
place!' he thought, and he
ran off and found the tree. It
looked easy to climb inside.

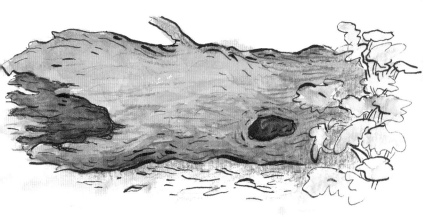

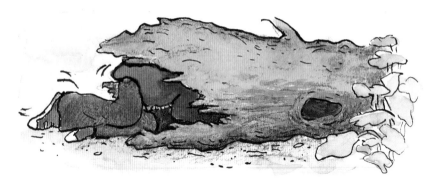

Getting into the tree wasn't as easy as he remembered. In fact, it was a bit of a squash.

'I must have been *much* smaller and younger, last time I got in here!' Dylan thought.

He kept very still and quiet.

He heard Mum shout, 'Coming, ready or not!'

He heard her find Dad.

He heard Mum find Shelley.

Dylan smiled to himself. They had no idea where he was.

He heard them come up to his tree.

Then he heard them go past. Their
footsteps sounded quieter and quieter.

'I've won!' he thought.

Now was the time to get out of the
tree and surprise them.

He tried to pull himself out. But he
couldn't move his arms properly.

He tried to wriggle out. That didn't work.

There was a little hole in the tree. He tried to push against it.

It was no good. He was stuck.

'Help! *Help!* HELP!' he called.

Then as loud as he could, he yelled,

He heard the sound of footsteps running back.

'I'm in here!' he shouted.

'What are you doing in there?' said his mum. 'Get out!'

'I can't! I'm stuck!' Dylan wailed.

His mum
p-u-l-l-e-d, but
it was no good.

His dad pushed.
It made no difference.
'I'm stuck!' Dylan wailed. 'Get me out!'

Get him out!

Only Dustbin was quiet. He was
chewing his stick and thinking.

Suddenly he had an idea.
Ding!
He trotted up to the tree.
He gave it a quick sniff.

He gave it a LONG look.

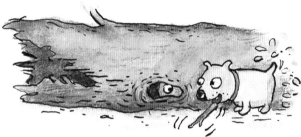

Then, calmly and quietly, he
started to chew.

It was old wood. It was rotten wood – and Dustbin had very sharp teeth. But still it wasn't easy.

Crunch, crunch, crunch, he went with his sharp white teeth.
Munch, munch, munch, he went.
Then *chew, chew, chew* and BITE!

Now there was a much bigger hole
in the tree, and with a wriggle ... and a
squiggle ... and a little bit of help ...
Dylan was free.

His mum, his dad and his sister hugged him.

But Dylan gave his biggest hug to Dustbin.

'You're the best dog in the world! he said. 'And I'm going to get you a fantastic present.'

The next day, the other dogs heard
how Dustbin had saved Dylan.

They were now much kinder to
Dustbin.

All the dogs had *something* to say,
but Dustbin had only one thing to say
to them:

About the author

I had a dog. He loved sticks – and I loved him. So I decided to put him in a story. The characters in my stories are made up, but they often *start* with someone from real life.

Dustbin is a *bit* like my dog. He's in three stories now. He's the hero of this one but he is also in two Treetop stories about Shelley Holmes, Dylan's sister. Like Dustbin, you could sniff them out and track them down – but if you find them, *don't* chew them!